FROGMORE HOUSE

and

THE ROYAL MAUSOLEUM

ROYAL COLLECTION TRUST

Written by Jane Roberts

Royal Collection Trust /

© HM Queen Elizabeth II 2018

First published by Royal Collection Trust 1997

Second revised edition reprinted 2005, 2006, 2008, 2011, 2012, 2013, 2018

010227/18

Find out more about the Royal Collection at
www.royalcollection.org.uk

ISBN 978 1 902163 25 3

British Library Cataloguing in Publication Data:
A catalogue record for this book is available from the British Library.

Production by Debbie Wayment

Printed in England by Typecast Colour

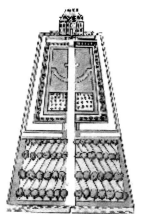

Above: Detail from a map of the Shaw and Frogmore estates in 1697, showing the west front of Frogmore House, with formal gardens.

Front cover: The west front of Frogmore House from the lake.

Back cover: The Royal Mausoleum from the east.

For conservation reasons, the levels of light in Frogmore House are kept relatively low. Pictures and works of art are also frequently lent from the Royal Collection to exhibitions all over the world. The arrangement of objects and paintings may therefore occasionally vary from that given in this guidebook. Visitors are asked to observe the 'Private' notices in the gardens, and to refrain from touching objects on view in the house and mausoleum.

For ticketing and booking information for Frogmore House, please see www.royalcollection.org.uk for more details, or contact the Ticket Sales and Information Office at
+44 (0)303 123 7305
Find out more about the Royal Collection Shop at
www.royalcollectionshop.co.uk

CONTENTS

HISTORY OF THE FROGMORE ESTATE   5

FROGMORE HOUSE:

     HISTORY AND ARCHITECTURE   8

     ROOM GUIDE

         The Entrance and Oak Room   11

         The Hall   12

         The Staircase   12

         The Cross Gallery   13

         Queen Mary's Flower Room   14

         The Black Museum   16

         The Duchess of Kent's Sitting Room   16

         The Green Pavilion   18

         The Charlotte Closet   21

         The Colonnade   23

         The Victoria Closet   26

         The Mary Moser Room   27

         The Duchess of Kent's Drawing Room   28

         The Britannia Room (formerly The Duchess of Kent's Dining Room)   30

THE GARDENS   33

THE ROYAL MAUSOLEUM   40

The Duchess of Kent's Sitting Room

History of the Frogmore Estate

The Frogmore estate first came into royal ownership in the mid-sixteenth century but it was held by a succession of Crown tenants for the following 250 years. It formed a substantial enclave between the Great Park and Little (now Home) Park of Windsor, directly bordering the old public road between Windsor and Old Windsor. No doubt it was the close proximity of the estate to the Castle that prompted its purchase by the Crown, for although low-lying and marshy (as its name suggests), its perimeter lies less than a mile from the southern façade of the Castle. One of the scenes in Shakespeare's play *The Merry Wives of Windsor* is set in a 'field near Frogmore'.

By the late seventeenth century the Aldworth family held the Crown leases of both the Frogmore and the adjoining Shaw estates, consisting of 250 acres in all. Their Windsor land-holdings were shown in a plan made in 1697, in the corner of which was a view of the new house at Frogmore, built for Anne Aldworth and her husband Thomas May *c.*1680 (see p. 2). However, following the departure of the Mays *c.*1685 and the death of Anne's brother William Aldworth in 1700, his children were forced to move to the smaller house to the north-west, Little Frogmore. After the departure of the Aldworth family, the larger house - Great Frogmore - was leased to the Duke of Northumberland (1665-1716), the natural son of Charles II and the Duchess of Cleveland. Following the death of the Duchess of Northumberland in 1738 the Great Frogmore estate passed through several hands including those of Horace Walpole's brother Edward (1706-1754), second son of the Prime Minister Sir Robert Walpole, until in 1792 it was purchased for Queen Charlotte (1744-1818), consort of George III (1738-1820).

However, the first property at Frogmore to be acquired for Queen Charlotte was the small adjoining estate immediately to the north-west, Little Frogmore. General William (later 3rd Earl) Harcourt, a loyal servant and friend of both the King and Queen, obtained the Crown lease of this property for the Queen in June 1790. The small house on this estate was used as a retreat by the Queen and her daughters; it was renamed Amelia Lodge after her youngest child, Princess Amelia, born in 1783. After additions and alterations to both the house (which at one stage was to be totally rebuilt) and the garden, Queen Charlotte looked forward to enjoying her 'little Paradise' and 'sweet retirement' at Amelia Lodge.

But the Queen's acquisition of the larger - Great Frogmore - estate in 1792 led to the amalgamation of the gardens of the two Frogmore estates and the demolition of Amelia Lodge, which was located just to the north of the surviving stable block of Frogmore House. The Queen's attention now passed to Frogmore House, which was altered and gradually extended. In the following year Queen Charlotte noted: 'I mean this place to furnish me with fresh amusements every day'. And as the diarist Fanny Burney recorded, the Queen spent most mornings at Frogmore, delighting in its quiet and ease and rarely returning to the Castle before dinner.

At the Queen's death in 1818 her Windsor estates passed to her eldest unmarried daughter, Princess Augusta (1768-1840), although most of the contents of Frogmore House were sold for the benefit of all her daughters in a series of auctions at Christie's in 1819. The Shaw estate had been reunited with the Frogmore estates in 1806 when Queen Charlotte acquired the Crown lease; thereafter her land-holding at Windsor amounted to nearly 350 acres, only 150 acres less than the total extent of the Home Park at this date

In March 1841 the leases of the Frogmore and Shaw estates were bought by the Crown from Princess Augusta's executors for £12,000, and by the end of the year the estates had been formally annexed to the royal domain at Windsor, by Act of Parliament. Since that time Frogmore House and grounds have enjoyed a similar status to that of other royal residences. In the same year another Act of Parliament provided for the setting up of a great new royal kitchen garden on part of the estate to the east. And in May 1841 Queen Victoria (1819-1901) - who had ascended the throne in 1837 - asked her widowed mother, the Duchess of Kent (1786-1861), if she would like to use Frogmore House and its pleasure grounds as her country home. The Duchess was born Princess Victoria of Saxe-Coburg and was therefore both aunt and mother-in-law to Queen Victoria's husband, Prince Albert (1819-1861). She resided at Frogmore for much of the following twenty years and is buried in a small mausoleum in the grounds to the west of the house. A second - and much larger - mausoleum was erected between 1862 and 1871 following the death of Prince Albert in 1861. Queen Victoria visited Frogmore regularly during her long widowhood and often worked on her papers there. Sitting in 'this dear lovely garden', she wrote in 1867, 'all is peace and quiet and you only hear the hum of the bees, the singing of the birds and the occasional crowing and cackling from the Poultry Yard! It does my poor excited, worried nerves good!'.

In July 1851 the public road that passed Frogmore between Windsor and Old Windsor was closed, as part of the Windsor Improvements. Although the road itself remains in use, within the Home Park, new public roads were constructed to the north and south. In the second half of the nineteenth century Frogmore House was used intermittently as the residence of different members of the Royal Family. The Princess of Wales (the future Queen Alexandra; 1844-1925) gave birth there to her first child (the Duke of Clarence and Avondale) in 1864; and from 1866 to 1872 Queen Victoria's third daughter, Princess Helena (Princess Christian; 1846-1923) and her husband Prince Christian of Schleswig-Holstein (1831-1917) lived in the house before moving to Cumberland Lodge.

During the reign of King Edward VII (1901-10) Frogmore was used by the King's son and daughter-in-law, the future King George V (1865-1936) and Queen Mary (1867-1953) who took a close interest in the house and grounds. As Duke and Duchess of York, King George VI (1895-1952) and Queen Elizabeth (1900-2002) spent part of their honeymoon at Frogmore in 1923.

The gardens were first opened to the public by King George VI in aid of the Queen's District Nurses. By command of Her Majesty The Queen the principal rooms of the house were opened for the first time in the summer of 1990. Although no longer a royal residence, the house and gardens at Frogmore are frequently used by the Royal Family.

Queen Charlotte, Princess Elizabeth and Princess Augusta, portrayed by Henry Edridge in the gardens of Frogmore House in the first decade of the nineteenth century

Frogmore House: History and Architecture

Little is known of the early buildings at Frogmore. The present house is essentially that erected for Anne Aldworth and her husband Thomas May *c*.1680, almost certainly to the designs of his uncle, Hugh May (1621-1684), who was Charles II's architect at Windsor. May's house was a handsome seven-bay brick edifice with pedimented entrance front on the east side and formal garden to the west (see p. 2). The remarkable wall-paintings on the staircase were almost certainly commissioned by the Duke of Northumberland around thirty years later. The existing stable block was also added at this time, *c*.1710. The house acquired by Queen Charlotte in 1792 was thus over a hundred years old. Although it had been continuously occupied and was in generally sound condition, a number of alterations were required to make it fit for the use of the Royal Family. However, Queen Charlotte never used the house as a residence, but rather as a retreat, for daytime visits. The architect James Wyatt (1746-1813) was employed by the Queen to convert the house for royal use. Wyatt had earlier been asked to prepare designs for the transformation of Amelia Lodge by the addition of gothick towers at the corners. His object at Frogmore House (and earlier at Amelia Lodge) was to create a modern 'Trianon' or retreat, where the Queen and her daughters could enjoy their favourite pastimes - painting, drawing, japanning and needlework, reading, music and above all 'botanising' - in privacy and tranquillity. This was

The west front of Frogmore House in 1793

achieved by the extension of the second floor and the addition of single-storey pavilions to north and south of the west (garden) front, linked by an open colonnade; these works were completed by May 1795. In 1804 the wings were enlarged by the addition of a tall bow room and a low room beyond, to make a Dining Room and Library at the south end and matching rooms at the north. Internally Wyatt gave the rooms a veneer of crisp neoclassical ornament, adding new chimneypieces and altering the staircase, though without drastically altering the seventeenth-century groundplan.

A partial record of the interior of the house as furnished for Queen Charlotte is contained in W.H. Pyne's *History of the Royal Residences* published in 1819, the year after the Queen's death. Pyne's illustrations, two of which were issued in 1817, clearly show Queen Charlotte's taste for elegant simplicity and also demonstrate the skill and ingenuity with which her daughters, in particular Princess Elizabeth (1770-1840), contributed to the decorations.

The inventory of the contents of Frogmore made soon after Princess Augusta's death indicates that few changes were made during her time there. However, during the two following decades the Duchess of Kent modernised and substantially redecorated the house, using it regularly until her death. A series of hand-coloured photographs in the Royal Photograph Collection records the appearance of the interior in 1861.

Early in the twentieth century Queen Mary was instrumental in arranging Frogmore as (in her own words) 'a "family" souvenir museum as well as a museum of "bygones" and of interesting odds and ends'. The appearance of the house in 1939 is recorded in a further series of photographs. These records were made on the eve of the transformation of the house to accommodate members of the Royal Household who were evacuated to Frogmore from their homes in London in wartime.

Since the 1870s the house has suffered serious problems with damp and dry rot. Bad outbreaks in the 1920s and 1930s even led to consideration of the suggestion that most of the building should be demolished; further serious outbreaks in the 1970s again threatened the existence of the house. The extensive restoration undertaken in the 1980s provided the opportunity to rearrange and redecorate certain rooms in order to illustrate the principal phases of the house's occupation from the early eighteenth to the mid-twentieth century. The wall-paintings in the Staircase Hall were uncovered in the course of the restoration campaign.

The Staircase Hall with the wall-painting of Dido sacrificing, *attributed to Louis Laguerre*

Guide to the Rooms

THE ENTRANCE AND OAK ROOM

Approaching from the south-east, the visitor can clearly see the extent of the alterations and additions made by James Wyatt to Frogmore in the 1790s. Externally, this work transformed a plain seven-bay late seventeenth-century brick house into an elegant stuccoed and painted villa by heightening the centre block and enlarging the balancing wings to north and south. The prominent stone porte cochère was added for the Duchess of Kent in the 1840s.

Having passed through the inner glass doors into the Hall, the visitor bears left into the Oak Room. In the seventeenth-century house this panelled room was known as the Parlour and the door leading into it from the Hall was closer to the Entrance. Wyatt moved the doorway to its present position, opposite the bottom of his new stairs, and was probably responsible for the partial re-arrangement of the old oak panelling. Despite these changes, the early character of the room remains intact.

Either during Queen Charlotte's time at Frogmore (1792-1818) or in that of her daughter Princess Augusta (1818-40), the Parlour became a billiard room. In the later nineteenth and early twentieth centuries it was used as an office. The room is now hung with nineteenth-century engraved portraits of members of the Royal Family including Queen Victoria, Prince Albert and six of their children (on the north wall); Prince and Princess Christian (above the doors opposite); and the Duchess of Kent (between the windows). There is also a small photographic display concerning the early history of the house and the discovery of the wall-paintings on the staircase in 1983-4.

Above the overmantel glass hangs a view of Windsor Castle from the south-east by Johannes Vorsterman. Although it is not an entirely faithful depiction, the view gives an impression of the appearance of the area between Frogmore and Windsor *c*.1680, at the time of the building of May's new house. Either side of the doorway are placed a pair of painted Windsor benches with George III's cypher on the back. The curtains are of late Victorian crimson chenille and the brightly coloured 'Turkey' carpet has been re-woven from a design of *c*.1860.

The Hall

In the original house a door directly opposite the Entrance led from the Hall into the Dining Room beyond. This opening was closed by Wyatt but its position is marked by a tall niche containing a plaster bust of George III after John Bacon. The stone and slate floor also dates from Wyatt's time. Either side of the door to the Oak Room hang two late seventeenth-century landscapes by Gerard van Edema, that on the right showing the Thames valley from Richmond Hill. Beneath them stand a pair of early nineteenth-century marble-topped side tables. On the left-hand table there is a marble bust of Princess Beatrice (1857-1944) in 1864 modelled by Princess Louise (1848-1939), respectively the fifth and fourth daughters of Queen Victoria. On the right-hand table is a bust of Prince Frederick William of Hesse (1870-1873), the son of Queen Victoria's second daughter, Princess Alice, attributed to Benedikt König. Underneath the tables are a pair of late seventeenth-century Japanese Arita vases and covers. The sculpture in the window bay is by William Scoular and depicts the sleeping figure of the infant Princess Elizabeth of Clarence (1820-1821), second daughter of William IV and Queen Adelaide.

The Staircase

The main staircase in the late seventeenth-century house rose anti-clockwise from the right of the front door round the walls of the stair well. The present staircase dates from 1794 when Wyatt replaced the original stairs with one of 'Imperial' design, consisting of a single flight rising centrally between a pair of crisply detailed Corinthian columns and branching at the first landing: this design, much favoured by Wyatt, was first used by him at Heaton Hall, Manchester, in 1772.

In the early eighteenth century, probably during the occupancy of the Duke of Northumberland (1709-16), the walls of the Staircase Hall were decorated with a cycle of murals, the subjects taken from Virgil's *Aeneid*. These were covered over before 1760 and were only re-discovered in 1983-4 during repairs to the stair well. The main panels, framed by illusionistic columns, represent *Aeneas and his Family leaving Troy* (on the west wall) and *Dido sacrificing* (on the north wall). The central figure in the scene on the south wall, representing *The Meeting of Aeneas and Venus*, has been badly damaged: before the main vertical strip was removed it appears that an unsuccessful attempt may have been made to remove the square of plaster containing Venus's head. The artist responsible for the paintings was probably the French decorative painter, Louis Laguerre (1663-1721), best known in England for his work at Chatsworth, Blenheim and Burghley. The damaged areas have been painted in a dark terracotta colour; a curtain conceals the largest area of paint loss on the north wall.

On the window ledges stand two black marble models of Egyptian obelisks by J. Maw; they were presented to William IV in 1832. The well and hall are lit by three early nineteenth-century bronzed and gilt brass hexagonal lanterns which are probably original to the house. The stair carpet reproduces an early nineteenth-century design; the pattern echoes as closely as possible the description of the needlework-bordered runner noted in the 1841 inventory.

Detail of the stair carpet rewoven to match the original

THE CROSS GALLERY

The Gallery spans the breadth of the house at first floor level. Although it was a feature of the original building, the present wall decoration - six panels of painted flower garlands suspended across illusionistic windows, alternating with nine narrower panels of flowers and paper cut-outs in the Etruscan style - was created in the 1790s by Princess Elizabeth, third daughter of George III and Queen Charlotte. This Princess, a gifted amateur artist, was also responsible for the Chinoiserie decoration of two further rooms at Frogmore, neither of which has survived intact although fortunately both were illustrated by Pyne.

Panels decorated by Princess Elizabeth in the Cross Gallery

The fitted Brussels carpet in the Caucasian style is from a design of 1850. The flowered chintz used for the chair covers and curtains is a modern reprint of a mid-Victorian pattern and the cotton lace is a reproduction of a nineteenth-century design of the kind known to have been here in 1861.

Most of the furniture, notably the two early nineteenth-century bow-fronted satinwood commodes with marble tops, the double-bowed amboyna cabinet and the four allegorical plaster statuettes in the niches at either end, has been arranged as it was in 1861. The marble bust on the left, by Mary Thornycroft (1814-1895), is of Prince Alfred (1844-1900), second son of Queen Victoria; that on the right, by William Behnes (1795-1864), is of Queen Victoria as a child. The porcelain vases are mid-nineteenth-century German, with the exception of the large blue vase which is Danish, c.1860. The pair of Chamberlain's Worcester oval jardinières on tables at either end were given to the Duchess of Kent on her birthday (17 August) in 1827, probably by her daughters Feodore and Victoria.

The rooms leading off the Gallery (which are not open to the public) include the Duchess of Kent's Bedroom and Sitting Room and are among the apartments used by Queen Mary to house the Family Museum, a private collection of souvenirs and mementos acquired by or given to members of the Royal Family over the years. Queen Mary initiated this project in the 1920s and continued to add to the collection until her death in 1953.

QUEEN MARY'S FLOWER ROOM

Returning via the Staircase and Hall, the visitor proceeds past the foot of the North Stairs through a small doorway in the outer wall of the seventeenth-century house and into the first of the rooms added by Wyatt to the north, Queen Mary's Flower Room. Originally a waiting room, then a smoking room and briefly a bedroom, the room was among those arranged by Queen Mary in the 1920s and takes its name from the collection of mid- to late nineteenth-century wax and silk flowers under glass domes that are displayed here. These and the other furnishings of the room have been re-instated with the help of the 1939 photographs.

The chintz curtains (which are original to the room) and the carpet are of the 1930s. Glass walking sticks and a sword (probably Nailsea, mid-nineteenth century), a late nineteenth-century screen inset with panels of gold brocade, lacquer caddies and boxes (mainly early to mid-nineteenth century) and the enormously varied contents of the two grained mahogany display cabinets (formerly at Buckingham Palace), present a vivid picture of Queen Mary's taste. The watercolour of Windsor Castle is attributed to William Payne (1760-1830); in the foreground is an imaginary view of boats on the river Thames, painted before Wyatville's work on the Castle in the 1820s. The marbleised slate chimney-piece dates from the mid-nineteenth century.

Queen Mary's Flower Room in 1939

THE BLACK MUSEUM

This is the second room which has been re-instated according to Queen Mary's arrangement, again using photographs taken in 1939. It owes its sinister name to the notable collection of nineteenth-century black papier-mâché and lacquer assembled here by Queen Mary in a room previously used as a bedroom and dressing room. The display includes a wide variety of papier-mâché furniture dating from *c.*1820 to 1880. Some pieces are inlaid with irridescent chips of mother-of-pearl, others are painted or gilded and a few pieces are signed by the leading Victorian firm of papier-mâché makers, Jennens and Bettridge. The mahogany sideboard and the firescreen are early nineteenth century and the octagonal wine-cooler late eighteenth century. The patterned pink-ground carpet dates from the late nineteenth century. The chintz curtains are modern reproductions of those hanging in Queen Mary's day. As in the previous room, the pictures are suspended by copper wire from S-hooks, the hanging method used in Queen Mary's time.

THE DUCHESS OF KENT'S SITTING ROOM

This room and the matching one to the north (the Duchess of Kent's Drawing Room) were added by James Wyatt in 1804. In Queen Charlotte's day and during the occupancy of her daughter Princess Augusta it was known as the Bow Drawing Room. No pictorial record survives of its appearance at that date. The Duchess of Kent used the room as a sitting and writing room and it is in this guise that it has been re-created, using the evidence of surviving fabrics and of the hand-coloured photographs taken in 1861. The decoration combines sharp, almost discordant, colouring with the dense clutter of furniture and ornaments characteristic of the mid-Victorian period. During the Duchess of Kent's residence (1842-61) the house was thoroughly re-decorated and substantially re-furnished, this room on at least two occasions. The soft lilac colour of the walls and woodwork, picked out in gold, was a favourite of the Duchess and exactly replicates the original colour scheme. The bright yellow silk of the curtains and elaborate passementerie (tassels, edgings, braid, etc.) match the surviving but much decayed mid-nineteenth-century curtains. The inner cotton lace curtains, like those in the Cross Gallery, reproduce a nineteenth-century design. The Brussels 'Persian' carpet, with a repeat of over nine feet, copies the large and complicated design and elaborate colouring of the carpet shown here in 1861. Like the

The display of papier mâché in the Black Museum

curtains, enough of this carpet survived to serve as a model for an accurate re-weaving. Much of the furniture seen in the 1861 photographs has been re-instated, notably the pair of pier glasses and semi-elliptical pier tables. Other pieces from the Duchess's time include the early nineteenth-century cut-glass chandelier, the needlework upholstered chairs protected by lace covers, the walnut piano by Erard and the cluster of writing tables covered with ornaments (see p. 4).

Most of the portraits were here in the Duchess's time. On the right wall are Queen Victoria and Prince Albert by John Partridge, and a small portrait of Prince Arthur (1850-1942), third son of Queen Victoria, by Corden after Winterhalter. Over the doors on the fireplace wall are portraits of the Princess Royal (1840-1901), eldest daughter of Queen Victoria, and the Prince of Wales, later King Edward VII (1841-1910), both by John Lucas and given to the Duchess of Kent by her daughter, Queen Victoria, in 1844. On the left wall are the Duke of Brabant, later King Leopold II of the Belgians (1835-1909) and the Count of Flanders (1837-1905), at either side of Princess Charlotte of Belgium, later Empress of Mexico (1840-1927). The last three paintings were copied, by Matthieu Fry and J. van Severdonck, after Winterhalter's portraits of the Duchess of Kent's nephews and niece, the children of her brother King Leopold I of the Belgians (1790-1865). The clock on the chimneypiece, by Julien Le Roy, Paris, of *c*.1850, belonged to the Duchess. The elephant-head vases either side are English (Minton) copies of an eighteenth-century Sèvres model. On the pier tables opposite are a pair of German (Ludwigsburg) gilt porcelain vases, *c*.1815, containing artificial flowers under glass domes, flanked by two pairs of Empire candelabra.

THE GREEN PAVILION

This is the only room on the public route which has been returned to its appearance in Queen Charlotte's time. Unlike the other rooms at Frogmore shown in Pyne's *Royal Residences*, it has undergone no significant changes since 1818 and Wyatt's characteristically crisp detailing of cornice, dado and chimneypiece remain largely intact. During the restoration campaign in the 1980s the walls were painted a brilliant green - from which the room takes its name - to match the remnants of the original colour found in the frieze. The lavish hang of the curtains, which contain over 400 yards of material, is copied from Pyne's view of the room (see p. 21); the pattern of the chintz is taken from a design of *c*.1804.

Of the furnishings shown by Pyne, only the cylindrical glass chandelier and the pair of small semi-circular side tables either side of the door to the Colonnade remain in the Royal Collection. The table tops, like those of the pier tables in the preceding room, are inset with flower watercolours and may have been executed by Princess Elizabeth. On the tables stand two groups of Chinese famille verte vases, c.1700, and below are a pair of Chinese beaker vases of about the same date. The four late eighteenth-century Indian ivory chairs with gilt decoration and leopard's head arms belonged to Queen Charlotte, a noted collector of ivory furniture. The three tables and chairs in front of the windows are similar to those in Pyne's view, as are the arrangements of (silk) flowers in porcelain vases. The cabinet shown by Pyne on the opposite (east) wall is no longer in the Royal Collection and in its place stands one of a set of mahogany cabinets attributed to the royal cabinet-maker William Vile, made c.1763 and formerly at Kensington Palace. Resting on the cabinet is an ormolu and white marble clock with Derby porcelain figures, c.1780, which belonged to William IV. On the chimneypiece there are a pair of ormolu-mounted blue-john candle-vases, attributed to Matthew Boulton, c.1770; a pair of Chelsea gold anchor figures of dwarfs and a Louis XVI ormolu mantel clock mounted with Wedgwood plaques. The carpet, similar to that shown by Pyne, is English and dates from the late eighteenth century.

Many of the paintings of Queen Charlotte's children recorded by Pyne are no longer in the Royal Collection and their places have been taken by other family portraits, some of which belonged to the Queen. On the chimney wall are Frederica (1752-1782) and Charles (1741-1816), Duke and Duchess of Mecklenburg-Strelitz, second brother and sister-in-law of Queen Charlotte, and the Queen's elder brother Adolphus Frederick, Duke of Mecklenburg-Strelitz (1738-1794), all by J.G. Ziesenis (1716-1776). Facing the window is an equestrian portrait of George III after Beechey and at either side portraits on copper of King George III and Queen Charlotte by Johann Zoffany (1733/4-1810); below these are portraits of the Queen's parents Charles (1708-1752) and Elizabeth (1713-1761), Duke and Duchess of Mecklenburg-Strelitz, by Daniel Woge.

To the left of the double doors to the Colonnade hangs a portrait by P.E. Stroehling (1768-c.1826) of Prince Augustus, Duke of Sussex (1773-1843), fourth son of George III, in the uniform of Colonel of the Loyal North Britons. This may be the picture seen in Pyne's view of the room. Above it is a portrait of William Henry, Duke of Gloucester (1743-1805), younger brother of George III, and over the door is a cheerful likeness of Princess Augusta, second daughter of George III; both portraits are

The Colonnade from the Green Pavilion

The Green Pavilion in 1817, reproduced in Pyne's Royal Residences *(published 1819)*

after Beechey. The Princess, who inherited Frogmore on her mother's death, used the Green Pavilion as a dining room. Thereafter it became a breakfast room and between 1902 and 1910 it was used as a school room by the future Kings Edward VIII and George VI.

THE CHARLOTTE CLOSET

In Queen Charlotte's time this may have been the room known as the Princess Royal's Closet. In his *Royal Residences* Pyne noted that a room of this name at Frogmore contained drawings of wild animals by the Princess Royal (Charlotte Augusta Matilda, 1766-1828), a talented amateur artist like her

Ludwigsburg porcelain plate decorated by George III's eldest daughter, Charlotte, Queen of Württemberg, 1813

younger sister Elizabeth. In 1797 the diarist Joseph Farington had noted sixty drawings by the Princess at Frogmore. Forty-five of the surviving drawings by the Princess, in their original frames (some still bearing the label of the carver Edward Wyatt) and glazing with black and gold surrounds, have now been reassembled here; they bear dates between August 1792 and May 1795. The Princess's drawings are based on engravings by seventeenth- and eighteenth-century artists such as Wenceslaus Hollar, Nicholaes Berchem, Francis Barlow, J.E. Ridinger and J.H. Mortimer.

The Princess was also responsible for the painted decoration on some of the porcelain in this room, including seven medallions (six painted with the heads of Emperors, one with birds in a landscape), two vases and a plate; the base of each piece is inscribed by the Princess with her initials and a date, between 1811 and 1816. The porcelain was made in the factory at Ludwigsburg (near Stuttgart), the Princess's home following her marriage in 1797 to the Hereditary Prince (later King) of Württemberg. Among the pieces of furniture displayed here, all of which date from the late eighteenth or early nineteenth century, there is a small oval table, the top inset with a drawing by the Princess Royal, and a box inset with a porcelain plaque decorated by the Princess. In the centre of the chimney piece there is a French ormolu clock dating from the early nineteenth century; at either side are pairs of ormolu-mounted blue-john candle-vases of the late eighteenth century and lapis and gilt-bronze candlesticks of the mid-nineteenth century. The carved detail around the doorcases is echoed in the gilt-bronze decoration on the grey marble chimneypiece and the colour scheme continues that of the Green Pavilion. The Brussels carpet is re-woven from a design of *c*.1830.

THE COLONNADE

James Wyatt designed the Colonnade as an open loggia on the garden front of Frogmore House, connecting the new rooms added to north and south. It was periodically used in Queen Charlotte's day as an informal setting for plays and concerts (see p. 34). By 1818 the Colonnade had been enclosed by French windows and in the Duchess of Kent's time it assumed a characteristically Victorian aspect, combining sculpture, flowers and lavish upholstery. The elaborate chintz curtains and fitted Brussels carpet have been reproduced with the assistance of the 1861 photographs and documented designs of the period.

The mid-nineteenth-century wire-work plant stands shown in these photographs have perished and in their place there are a set of green-painted stands with rope decoration made by Tatham, Bailey and Sanders in 1815; these may have been at Frogmore in Queen Charlotte's time. The plaster casts of Queen Victoria's nine children, all inscribed with their names, are ranged along the walls. The casts were taken from the marble figures by Mary Thornycroft, now at Osborne House. Mrs Thornycroft, the daughter of the sculptor John Francis, was the wife of Thomas Thornycroft, sculptor of Boadicea on Westminster Bridge, and mother of another well-known sculptor, Hamo Thornycroft. The busts in the centre of the west wall represent the Queen and Prince Albert; they are supported by rococo brackets possibly designed by John Cheere. The busts on the facing wall portray King Leopold I of the Belgians (by Guillaume Geefs) and his wife, Queen Louise (after Geefs).

The backs of the nine caned maplewood chairs are carved with the initials of Princess Helena, third daughter of Queen Victoria, and of her husband Prince Christian, who lived at Frogmore in the late 1860s before taking up residence at Cumberland Lodge in the Great Park. In front of the windows is a pair of silver-mounted curling stones presented to Prince Albert on his first visit to Scotland in 1842. The late nineteenth-century oak table (supporting the cast of Princess Beatrice in a shell) was made by A. and F. Halliday of Eton from a piece of the old flagstaff of the Round Tower.

Centre pages: Charles Wild's view of the west front of Frogmore House, painted for Pyne's Royal Residences *(1819)*

THE VICTORIA CLOSET

This small room, a pendant to the Charlotte Closet but distinguished by its unusual vaulted ceiling, now contains a number of works of art executed in the nineteenth century by three generations of the Royal Family. Above the doors are two landscapes by Victoria, Duchess of Kent, painted during her first marriage to the Prince of Leiningen. The Duchess's daughter, Queen Victoria, gave her drawing of a girl holding a hat (on the adjoining wall) to her uncle, King George IV, for his last birthday, in August 1829. To the left of the alcove are copies by Queen Victoria of two watercolours by Carl Haag. On the facing wall is the Queen's copy of Landseer's drawing of Archie and Annie Macdonald, the children of John Macdonald, formerly Prince Albert's *jäger* (ghillie) at Balmoral, but from 1848 Keeper of the Queen's Kennels at Windsor; the Queen's drawing is dated 1851.

The remaining pictures in the room are by the most talented of Queen Victoria's children, Victoria, Princess Royal, who in 1858 married Frederick William, Crown Prince of Prussia, later Emperor Frederick III of Germany. In the alcove is her oil painting after Rembrandt's portrait of his mother. The original hangs in the State Apartments at Windsor Castle; the copy was painted while the Princess was visiting Queen Victoria at Windsor in 1878. To the right of this painting is a watercolour of a scene from Shakespeare's play *Richard II*, painted in 1857. The three still lifes (above the fitted cupboards) were painted

The Princess Royal's 1862 design for a porcelain plaque incorporating the initials of her parents, Victoria and Albert

in the early 1870s. The two watercolour designs with the V and A monogram were sent from Germany by the Princess in 1862. They were used as models for the decoration of a group of Berlin porcelain plaques which were subsequently mounted on the amboyna-wood secretaire in this room. The secretaire, which was made in the 1820s, formed part of the furnishings of the room in Windsor Castle in which Prince Albert died in 1861 and which was thereafter dedicated to the Prince's memory by his grieving widow.

THE MARY MOSER ROOM

Mary Moser (1744-1819), a renowned flower painter and one of the foundation members of the Royal Academy, was commissioned by Queen Charlotte to decorate this newly-built room with garlands of flowers simulating an arbour open to the skies. The paintings were probably executed in the mid-1790s and apparently cost £900. The Queen, whose favourite room this was said to have been, commanded that it should thereafter be known by the artist's name. Mrs Moser's six framed paintings may have been painted a little earlier for Amelia Lodge. Likewise, the large painting set into the east wall, with its emphasis on the Order of the Garter, appears to have been commissioned for another setting at Windsor, either in the Castle itself or in The Queen's Lodge, the main residence of the Royal Family at Windsor in the late eighteenth century.

The notable chimneypiece, with frieze carved to simulate drapery, is attributed to the sculptor Richard Westmacott the Elder. The furniture, which includes a pair of white-painted commodes with marble tops, a revolving four-tier bookstand and two rosewood tables, is mainly of Queen Charlotte's period, though the room arrangement and features such as the red striped case covers of the chairs and sofa are of the Duchess of Kent's time. During the Duchess's occupation the room was used as a sitting room by her faithful Lady-in-Waiting, Lady Augusta Bruce. The crimson silk damask curtains, patterned with roses and ribbons, are nineteenth century and the Axminster carpet woven with flowers is attributed to Thomas Whitty, c.1780. The pair of cut-glass lustres and the ormolu mantel clock date from the 1820s.

The plaster bust of the Duchess of Kent in the far corner is after William Theed and the two marble busts of children are by Mary Thornycroft: the bust to the left of the chimneypiece portrays Prince and Princess Christian's son, Albert, Duke of Schleswig-Holstein (1869-1931), who was born at Frogmore; facing the window is a portrait bust of the Princess Royal, dated 1846.

Detail of the east wall of the Mary Moser Room

THE DUCHESS OF KENT'S DRAWING ROOM

Built by Wyatt as a Dining Room for Queen Charlotte, this room is shown by Pyne in 1819 simply furnished with mahogany table and chairs and lit by glass chandeliers and silver sconces; it matched the Bow Drawing Room (now The Duchess of Kent's Sitting Room) to the north. The marble chimneypiece carved with masks and vines was purchased in Rome in 1795 by the Duke of Sussex, sixth son of George III, from the eccentric English sculptor John Deare. The doorcases and ceiling were enriched in Princess Augusta's time but the main features of Wyatt's oval room are clearly visible beneath the present French-inspired grey, gold and silver decoration, commenced in 1860 for the Duchess of Kent. After the Duchess's death, the room was occasionally used as a ballroom. For a period before the Second World War, when at Queen Mary's suggestion Frogmore was used as an outpost of the Royal Archives, the room served as a research room.

The Duchess of Kent's Drawing Room

On the south (chimney) wall are portraits of the Duchess of Kent's brother and sister-in-law, King Leopold and Queen Louise of the Belgians, by Winterhalter. The Duchess's nephew - Prince Albert's elder brother - Duke Ernest II of Saxe-Coburg-Gotha (by John Lucas) and his wife Alexandrine (by Winterhalter) are the subjects of the portraits to left and right of the north (entrance) wall; in the centre of that wall is Beechey's portrait of Augusta, Duchess of Cambridge, sister-in-law of the Duchess of Kent and grandmother of Queen Mary.

The room is lit by a gilt-bronze chandelier of *c*.1820 and by six Wedgwood and gilt-bronze candelabra made in the late eighteenth century; four of these are supported by Regency giltwood torchères made for Carlton House. In the window bay is a Russian malachite tazza on Korgon porphyry base with gilt-bronze mounts; it was acquired by George IV for Windsor Castle. Either side of the chimneypiece is a pair of French late eighteenth-century satinwood and rosewood console tables with Wedgwood panels. The octagonal table of specimen woods at the east end of the room is attributed to George Bullock, *c*.1815.

On the chimneypiece are a pair of Minton porcelain vases with wistaria decoration, *c*.1860, and a French white marble mantel clock inset with Wedgwood plaques. On the centre tables are Parian-ware busts of Queen Victoria and Prince Albert and a framed photograph of Princess Frederica of Hanover.

THE BRITANNIA ROOM
(formerly The Duchess of Kent's Dining Room)

The original appearance of this room, built by Wyatt as a library for Queen Charlotte, can be judged from the view published in 1817 for Pyne's *Royal Residences*. At this date Queen Charlotte employed a full-time librarian, Edward Harding, and there were two further library rooms to the east and north-east of the Dining Room next door: the latter contained a Botanical Library and the former was known as the Small Library. Elsewhere in the house Queen Charlotte had a printing press and bindery. Shortly after the Queen's death in 1818, some 5,000 volumes from her library were sold at Christie's in a sale which lasted 23 days. Nominally the room remained a library until the Duchess of Kent took over the house in 1841 at which time it was converted into a Dining Room. The grey and gold scheme was completed after the Duchess's death by Queen Victoria and Prince Albert whose monogram with the date 1862 may be seen above the window on the garden side.

Following the decommissioning of H.M. Yacht *Britannia* in December 1997, The Duke of Edinburgh arranged a selection of items in this room to reflect the interior of the Royal Yacht. The mahogany table was made for *Britannia* while the Hepplewhite dining chairs and the four sideboards by Waring and Gillow were retained from the previous yacht *Victoria & Albert III*. The paintings include views of previous royal yachts from the past hundred years. On the end wall are three paintings recording events in the life of *Britannia*: her launch on Clydebank in 1953 (by N. Wilkinson); her return to London following her maiden voyage in 1954 (by L.A. Wilcox), and the Silver Jubilee Review in 1977 (by R.R. Fisher).

The two silver gilt vases, the Nelson and Collingwood Testimonials, were presented by the National Patriotic Fund to Vice Admiral Lord Collingwood and to Nelson's widow after the battle of Trafalgar in 1805. Both vases were purchased at auction by the Prince of Wales (subsequently King Edward VII) in 1898. The room is now regularly used by members of the Royal Family for charity functions.

Queen Charlotte's Library in 1817, later transformed as the Duchess of Kent's Dining Room

The wistaria-covered walls of the Gothic Ruin

The Gardens

Although the flat natural setting did not commend itself for the creation of a garden, the extensive grounds to the west of the house have provided the chief and enduring attraction of Frogmore to the Royal Family. Queen Charlotte's interest in botany was nurtured at Kew in the 1770s and 1780s and was given full rein at Frogmore where her garden was laid out with rare and unusual plants. She formed an extensive botanical library and flowers became a major theme in the decoration of the house.

The gardens were soon transformed from a series of geometric enclosures into a model of picturesque planning and planting. Work in the garden of Amelia Lodge commenced in 1790; in the following year there was considerable planting activity and by early 1792 4,000 new trees and shrubs had been introduced there. Before the acquisition of the Great Frogmore estate about £2,500 had been spent on the garden alone. A path was set out around the fields, a berceau (covered walk) was created and the tree-lined road leading to Shaw Farm was taken into the grounds and the road diverted to the west. This work was apparently supervised by the Reverend Christopher Alderson, rector of Eckington in Derbyshire and friend of the poet and gardener, William Mason. Major William Price (*c*.1750-1817), younger brother of Uvedale Price, the pioneer of the picturesque theory of landscaping, was also consulted late in 1790; he had been one of the King's Equerries in the 1780s and was appointed Vice-Chamberlain to the Queen in November 1792.

The Iron Bridge

After the acquisition of the adjoining estate of Great Frogmore in September 1792 the garden layout was totally re-thought.

The Frogmore Fête of 1795

The combined pleasure grounds occupied nearly 35 acres and included a stream leading to a canal stretching to the south-west of the house. The canal was incorporated as one arm of a meandering stream or lake; banks were created from the waste produced by the digging of the other arms and small pleasure buildings were added at strategic points. These new garden features included a Gothic Ruin (designed by Wyatt and Princess Elizabeth), a thatched Hermitage and a barn or garden ballroom (both designed by Princess Elizabeth) and an octagonal Gothic Temple of Solitude. Of these only the first survives, overlooking the lake, while the Temple of Solitude was replaced by the Duchess of Kent's mausoleum in the 1850s. Alderson is not mentioned at Windsor after 1792 and the large existing garden was evidently the responsibility of William Price alone.

In Queen Charlotte's day the gardens were used periodically for receptions and fêtes: the first fête was held in 1793 and was followed by a major celebration in 1795, by which time the first wave of work on the house was complete. The King's Jubilee in 1809 was the occasion for another grand fête, attended by upwards of 1,200 people. On this occasion there were fireworks and illuminations, 'an elegant supper' and a water pageant celebrating the triumph of Britannia. The temporary buildings erected for the occasion included a temple designed by Princess Elizabeth and executed by Wyatt (see page 48).

The grounds were maintained and greatly appreciated by both Princess Augusta and the Duchess of Kent. Among the new features added by the Duchess was the small circular colonnaded temple which became her mausoleum (see pp. 37-38). As the setting for both Prince Albert's and the Duchess of Kent's mausolea, the gardens at Frogmore remained especially sacred for Queen Victoria and the Royal Family. Many of the trees planted at this time have survived: on the lawn in front of the house is a fine Incense Cedar (*Libocedrus decurrens*), which was planted by the Duchess's son-in-law, Prince Hohenlohe, in March 1857, only four years after being introduced from California.

By the early twentieth century the gardens had become overgrown and the lawns were smothered in dense masses of evergreen. After the end of the First World War Queen Mary set about clearing and redesigning the gardens. Numerous flowering trees, shrubs and grasses, and some 200,000 bulbs, were introduced, and many ancient trees and plants were removed. In 1977 the Keeper of the Gardens in Windsor Great Park was asked to look critically at the gardens with a view to their rejuvenation. At the same time numerous donations of trees and shrubs were made in commemoration of Her Majesty's Silver Jubilee. This resulted in much new planting which is gradually maturing and adds considerably to the beauty and interest of the garden.

The Gothic Ruin

The following descriptions relate to the principal features in the grounds of Frogmore House. None of the buildings are open to the public.

Queen Victoria's Tea House

The Urns

The massive urns now flanking the Colonnade were moved to their present position earlier this century. They were carved by Joseph Harris of Bath *c.*1820.

Queen Victoria's Tea House

The brick and tiled Tea House was built for Queen Victoria in the south-eastern corner of the garden. This picturesque building, formed of two small rooms connected by a loggia, dates from 1869-70 and is probably the work of S.S. Teulon (1812-1873). In the summer the Queen would often work in a tent erected close to the Tea House.

Against the bank opposite the Tea House Queen Victoria erected a granite drinking fountain, inscribed 'In affectionate remembrance of John Brown, Queen Victoria's devoted personal attendant and friend, 1883'.

The Swiss Seat

This open timber hut, faced with split trunks arranged as gothic blind tracery, is probably identifiable with the 'Neat Swiss Seat' described as being erected near the lake in 1833.

The Duchess of Kent's Mausoleum

The mausoleum of Queen Victoria's mother, the Duchess of Kent, is situated on a mound above the Swiss Seat between two arms of the lake. It is a small circular building surrounded by columns with an upper chamber occupied by a full-length statue of the Duchess (by William Theed) and a lower burial chamber containing her sarcophagus. Work commenced in the late 1850s, under the direction of Prince Albert. The upper level of the building was intended to serve as a summer house during the Duchess's lifetime but work was still under way at the time of her death in March 1861. The building was erected to the designs of the Prince's artistic adviser, Professor Ludwig Gruner of Dresden (1801-1882), but the executant architect was A.J. Humbert (1822-1877). The design is partly inspired by Hawksmoor's mausoleum at Castle Howard (1729).

The Duchess of Kent's Mausoleum

Memorial Crosses

Two memorial crosses are located on the island close to the mausolea. That to Prince Albert's mentor Baron Stockmar (1787-1863) is close to the Royal Mausoleum, while that to Lady Augusta Stanley (née Bruce; 1822-1876), the devoted friend and servant of both the Duchess of Kent and Queen Victoria, faces the steps leading to the Duchess's Mausoleum.

The Indian Kiosk

The white marble kiosk was presented to Queen Victoria by Lord Canning after the capture of Lucknow in 1858 and the end of the Indian Mutiny. It is situated in the northern part of the garden.

The Indian Kiosk

The Gothic Ruin

This building was designed by James Wyatt with the assistance of Princess Elizabeth and was built in the 1790s. It was used by Queen Victoria as a breakfast or reading room. (See illustration on p. 35.)

The sundial

The sundial on the open ground to the south of the lake commemorates the election in 1831 of the Duchess of Kent's brother, Leopold of Saxe-Coburg, as King of the Belgians. It was formerly at Claremont House, Surrey, Leopold's home following his earlier marriage to Princess Charlotte of Wales, and was purchased by Queen Mary.

The Royal Mausoleum

The Royal Mausoleum is one of the most remarkable buildings of the Victorian age. It was built to contain the mortal remains of Prince Albert and of his widow Queen Victoria.

The idea for a mausoleum appears to have been inspired by the Gothic mausoleum erected at Claremont by Prince Leopold of Saxe-Coburg in memory of his young wife, Princess Charlotte (daughter of the Prince Regent), who died in childbirth in 1817. After the death in 1844 of Leopold's brother Duke Ernest I of Saxe-Coburg-Gotha, the Duke's sons, Albert and Ernest, made plans for a mausoleum at Coburg (executed by the architect Eberhardt) which would serve as a burial place for their father and members of their family. In 1860 Queen Victoria commented that the Coburg mausoleum was 'beautiful and so cheerful'. Leopold and Ernest's sister, Victoria, Duchess of Kent, had hoped to be buried there but was persuaded that an English place of burial was both more practical and more suitable. After her death in 1861 she was buried in the small mausoleum in Frogmore gardens described above.

These precedents explain how Queen Victoria and Prince Albert decided to make independent plans for their own place of burial, and to abandon the traditional burial places of the British Royal Family, in particular Westminster Abbey and St George's Chapel. It is clear that their decision was made many years before the Prince's premature death. Within four days of Prince Albert's death in December 1861 the Queen had chosen the site for the new mausoleum. This was to be in the south-western area of the garden, beyond the lake and a short distance to the west of the Duchess of Kent's mausoleum. It was surrounded by a large area of garden which was to be replanted and landscaped in an appropriate manner.

Once again the designs for the building were the responsibility of Ludwig Gruner with the assistance of A.J. Humbert, but members of the Prince's family - particularly Queen Victoria and their eldest child, the Princess Royal - were closely involved in all aspects of the planning, construction and ornamentation. The exterior of the mausoleum was inspired by Italian Romanesque buildings, while the ornamentation of the interior employed the style of the Italian Renaissance painter Raphael, considered by Prince Albert to be the greatest artist of all time.

Work commenced on the site in March 1862, the dome was turned by October, and the central part of the structure had progressed far enough to be consecrated in December although the decoration was only completed in August 1871. The cost of the mausoleum was borne entirely by Queen Victoria. However, the Prince of Wales made a substantial contribution to the original work and after his accession as King Edward VII in 1901 he paid for all the stained glass to be renewed and for the interior of the dome to be repainted; he also presented the large bronze lamps outside the entrance. As various tablets in the interior record, he commissioned these works in memory of Queen Victoria and other members of the Royal Family

THE EXTERIOR

The mausoleum is a symmetrical building, employing a Greek cross groundplan with an external diameter of 70 feet. It is oriented with the chancel in the west, the reverse of the usual ecclesiastical layout in which the chancel is at the east end. The walls are built of granite (from Aberdeen, Mull, Devon, Cornwall and Guernsey) and Portland stone and the roof is covered with Australian copper. At either side of the entrance are two bronze statues of angels bearing a sword and a trumpet, made by Georg Howaldt of Brunswick in 1878. Above the porch is a circular terracotta medallion of the head of Christ, sent from Germany by the Princess Royal, Crown Princess of Prussia. The steps in the upper flight leading to the porch are made of black Galway marble and the pavement of the porch is inlaid coloured marble. On the ceiling of the porch is a mosaic by the Venetian artist Antonio Salviati. The two urns on either side of the entrance, and others inside the building, were designed by Gruner and made at Göblitz in Saxony.

The outer entrance gates are of bronze and the inner ones of brass. Both sets were made by Potter & Sons of London, after designs by Gruner.

The interior of the Royal Mausoleum with the marble effigies of Prince Albert and Queen Victoria

The interior

The Tomb

In the centre of the mausoleum is the tomb of Queen Victoria and the Prince Consort. The Prince's remains were interred here on the completion of the tomb chest in 1868; they were joined by those of the Queen after her own death in January 1901.

The tomb was designed by Baron Carlo Marochetti (1805-1867). The recumbent marble effigies of the Queen and the Prince Consort were Marochetti's last works and were still in his studio - though complete - when he died. The effigy of the Queen was made at the same time as that of her husband, but was not brought to the mausoleum until after her funeral. Above the effigies hang the standards of the Queen and the Prince Consort, together with their crests, helms and swords. During their lives, these were located above the Queen's and Prince's stalls in St George's Chapel.

The sarcophagus is made from a single block of grey Aberdeen granite from the Cairngall quarries. It is said to be the largest block of flawless wrought granite in existence and is the fourth block quarried for the purpose, the first three attempts having ended in failure when flaws were discovered on the underneath of the stones after they had been detached. The tomb chest rests upon a base of black Belgian marble which had been promised for the mausoleum by King Leopold I of the Belgians, and was presented after his death in 1865 by his son, King Leopold II. The four bronze angels and other enrichments, also designed by Marochetti, were made by the firm of Barbedienne in Paris.

At the base of the tomb, on the Queen's side, is a small bronze cross resting on a Union Jack. This was a tribute to Queen Victoria from her daughter-in-law, Queen Alexandra.

The Central Octagon

The pavement and the walls of the Central Octagon are covered with inlaid coloured marbles from the United Kingdom, Italy, France, Greece, Portugal, Africa, and North America. The Portuguese marble, known as Emperor's Red, forms the general wall surface into which the other marbles are inlaid. It was a gift from the King of Portugal, who was a cousin of both the Queen and Prince Albert.

Within niches in each of the four piers supporting the dome are figures of Hebrew Kings and Prophets, each carved by a different Dresden sculptor. Starting from the left of the entrance, facing the tomb, these are: David, by Heinrich Bäumer; Isaiah by Hermann Hultzsch; Daniel by Gustav Kuntz; and Solomon by Friedrich Rentsch. The pilasters beneath the main arches were designed by Alessandro Mantovani of Rome and their capitals and bases were supplied by Barbedienne.

On the four spandrels above the statues are paintings of the four Evangelists by Nicola Consoni. The background is painted to resemble gold mosaic. Above them, on the eight panels at the base of the dome, pairs of angels hold wreaths of immortelles (everlasting flowers) surrounding the monogram of Victoria and Albert. These were painted by Pfänder from cartoons by Consoni.

The apex of the dome is 70 feet above the floor. The vaulting ribs are adorned with angels modelled by Hultzsch and worked in papier mâché by Parlby of London. The inner surface of the dome is decorated with angels bearing crowns and wreaths of immortelles on a background of clouds and gold stars. This design was the work of Ion Pace in 1909 and replaced an earlier one by Gruner which consisted of gold stars on a deep blue ground. Gruner's original windows of patterned glass made at Meissen were also replaced by Pace. Below the statues of the Kings and Prophets are three bronze wreaths, presented in memory of Queen Victoria shortly after her death. The donors were the Emperor Menelik of Ethiopia, the Captain and Officers of the Brazilian cruiser *Floriano,* which was on a special mission to London at the time, and 'Her Native Subjects of the District of Butterworth, Transkei'.

Each of the four tunnel-vaulted recesses opening off the Central Octagon has the status of a separate chapel. The walls and ceilings of each chapel - and of the ambulatory which skirts the inner wall of the mausoleum, linking each chapel - are decorated with paintings and reliefs.

The Entrance Chapel

From the entrance porch the visitor passes directly into the Entrance Chapel. On the ceiling of this chapel is a painting of the Apotheosis by Julius Frank from a cartoon by the Princess Royal. On either side of it, at the base of the vault, are bas reliefs which, like those in the other chapels, were conceived by Consoni, mainly after paintings by Raphael, modelled by Hermann Hultzsch at Dresden and cast in that town by

Wiessing. That on the left (facing the entrance) represents reaping, and that on the right sowing. On the wall above the entrance gates is a painting of the Cardinal Virtues by Consoni, from a fresco by Raphael in the Vatican. The Queen had asked for a representation of the Wise and Foolish Virgins for this spot; but Gruner pointed out that there was no composition by Raphael on this subject, and suggested the Cardinal Virtues instead. On each side of the entrance gates are paintings of the Apostles St Peter and St Paul by Consoni after a composition by Raphael. Below the cornice, on either side of the arches, are small circular medallions bearing allegorical figures by Pietro Galli of Rome. There are similar medallions in the other chapels. The painted grotesques around them, and elsewhere in the building, were designed by Gruner after Renaissance copies of antique Roman grotesques, and executed by the London firm of W. Homann.

The four chapels are linked by an outer corridor or ambulatory. The stained glass windows throughout the ambulatory were designed, like the other windows, by Pace, and replaced earlier windows by Gruner. The latter had consisted of angels playing musical instruments after compositions by Giovanni da Fiesole chosen by the Princess Royal. Pace's windows represent similar subjects. In the section of this ambulatory which leads in a clockwise direction from the Entrance Chapel (i.e. to the right facing the entrance) is a bust by Sir Edgar Boehm of Leopold, Duke of Albany, fourth son of Queen Victoria, who died in 1884 at the age of 30.

The Chapel of the Nativity

On the ceiling of this chapel, to the left (south) of the Central Octagon, is a painting of the Annunciation by Pfänder and Julius Frank after Raphael. Beneath it on the right is a bas relief of the Sacrifice of Isaac, and on the left another relief of the Sacrifice of Manoah. The painting of the Nativity on the main (south) wall is by Consoni, after a tapestry by Raphael.

In the centre of the chapel is a monument by Boehm to Princess Alice, Grand Duchess of Hesse (1843-1878), second daughter of Queen Victoria, who died of diphtheria shortly after her youngest daughter, May (1874-1878), had died of the same disease. She was the first of Queen Victoria's children to die and by a curious turn of fate the date of her death, 14 December, was the same as that of her father seventeen years earlier.

The next section of the ambulatory contains busts of Princess Alice's husband, Grand Duke Louis of Hesse (1837-1892), and of Prince Henry of Battenberg (1858-1896), husband of Princess Beatrice; the latter died of fever contracted during the Ashanti War in 1896. The group of Queen Victoria and the Prince Consort in Anglo-Saxon dress was carved by William Theed (1804-1891) in 1867. The Queen records in her diary that the idea for the group came from the Princess Royal. The pedestal is made from an antique fragment of African marble found in Rome; it is inscribed with a quotation from *The Deserted Village* by Oliver Goldsmith.

Prince Albert and Queen Victoria in Anglo-Saxon dress, by William Theed, 1867

The Chapel of the Altar

This chapel occupies the central recess or chancel area. On its ceiling is a painting of the Ascension by Pfänder from a cartoon by Consoni after a tapestry by Raphael. The bas reliefs beneath it are of Jonah (on the right) and of Samson at Gaza (on the left). Behind the altar is a painting of the Resurrection by Consoni, after a tapestry by Raphael. On the altar, which was designed by Gruner, is a bas relief of the Deposition by Galli. The sanctuary chairs on either side of the altar were designed by A.Y. Nutt (1847-1924, Assistant Architect and Surveyor at Windsor Castle), and presented by King Edward VII in 1905. The centre window above the altar shows Our Lord in Majesty holding the Book of Life, in which are inscribed the Greek letters alpha and omega. The sidelights contain groups of angels bearing musical instruments and censers. All were designed by Pace in 1905 and replaced earlier patterned glass by Gruner.

The ambulatory beyond this chapel contains a statue by Boehm of the Emperor Frederick III of Germany (1831-1888), husband of the Princess Royal, who died after a reign of only ninety days.

The Chapel of the Crucifixion

On the ceiling of this chapel, to the right of the Central Octagon, is a painting of the Carrying of the Cross by Julius Frank and Pfänder after Raphael. The bas reliefs beneath it are of the Brazen Serpent (on the right) and the Expulsion from Paradise (on the left). On the outer wall is a painting of the Crucifixion by Consoni.

In the centre of the chapel is a monument by Boehm to Edward, Duke of Kent, Queen Victoria's father. The Duke, who died in 1820, is buried in St George's Chapel, where this monument was originally placed by Queen Victoria in 1874; it was moved to Frogmore in 1950.

On one side of the chapel is the bronze head of an angel which fell from the Albert Memorial in Kensington Gardens during an air raid on the night of 1-2 October 1940, and was placed in the mausoleum by King George VI.

On the inner wall of the next section of the ambulatory, below the first urn, is a tablet erected to the memory of John Brown (1826-1883), Queen Victoria's Highland servant. Beyond this tablet stands a marble monument to Prince Christian Victor of Schleswig-Holstein (1867-1900), eldest son of Queen Victoria's third daughter, Princess Helena, the wife of Prince Christian of Schleswig-Holstein. Prince Christian Victor died on active service during the South African War. The monument, by Emil Fuchs (1866-1929), was commissioned by Queen Victoria but was not completed until a year after the Queen's death. It was originally placed in St George's Chapel and was moved to Frogmore in 1965.

THE ROYAL BURIAL GROUND (CLOSED TO THE PUBLIC)

The area to the south-west of the Royal Mausoleum was consecrated for use as a private burial ground in 1928. Among those buried here are three of Queen Victoria's children: Princess Helena (and her husband Prince Christian), Prince Arthur, Duke of Connaught (with his wife) and Princess Louise. In more recent times Prince William of Gloucester, Princess Alice, Countess of Athlone, and the Duke and Duchess of Windsor have also been buried here. The burial ground is dominated by the vast figure of Christ by the Swedish sculptor Laurits Rasmussen, presented by Queen Alexandra as a 'Tribute of love and affection to the best and greatest of Sovereigns and the kindest of mothers-in-law, from her ever grateful and most loving daughter-in-law, Alexandra, 1903'.

The water pageant at the Jubilee Fête at Frogmore, 1809, with decorations designed by Princess Elizabeth and James Wyatt

FURTHER READING

J. Cornforth, 'Frogmore House, Berkshire - I and II', *Country Life*, 16 August, pp. 46-51 and 23 August 1990, pp. 42-5

E. Darby and N. Smith, *The Cult of the Prince Consort*, London, 1983

O. Hedley, *Queen Charlotte*, London, 1975

H. Hobhouse, *Prince Albert: His Life and Work*, London, 1983

D. Jacques, *Georgian Gardens - The Reign of Nature*, London, 1990

W.H. Pyne, *The History of the Royal Residences*, London, 1819

G. Plumptre, *Royal Gardens*, London, 1981

J. Roberts, *Royal Artists*, London, 1987

J. Roberts, *A Royal Landscape. The Gardens and Parks of Windsor*, New Haven and London, 1997

N. Smith, 'Frogmore House before James Wyatt', *The Antiquaries Journal*, LXV, II, 1985, pp. 402-26

R. Strong, *Royal Gardens*, London, 1992